Saint Patrick
The Enlightener of Ireland

STORIES OF SAINTS FOR CHILDREN SERIES

8

Retold and illustrated by S.V. SBIERA

Saint Patrick
Bishop of Armagh,
Enlightener of Ireland
March 17

All people on Earth are God's children. God loves his children very much and cares for them.

That is why sometimes He gently intervenes to show His children the way to salvation. This is how it was with the ancestors of Irish people.

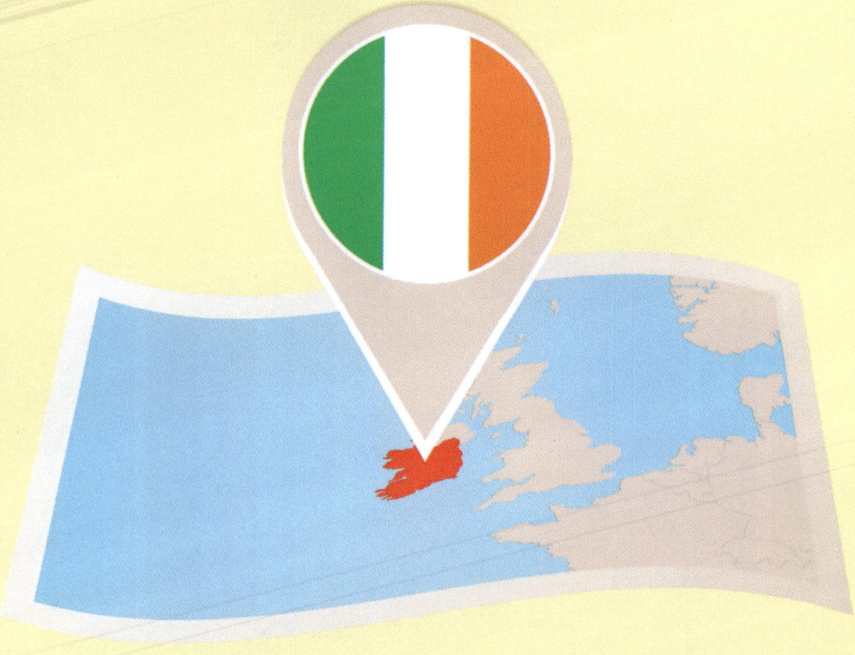

God loved these good people and sent Saint Patrick to teach them and show them the way to the Kingdom of Heaven. And now our story begins.

One thousand six hundred years ago during the Roman Empire in Britain, there lived a young man named Patrick.

Patrick was raised in a Christian family. His father, Calpurnius, was a deacon, and his grandfather was a priest.

Patrick spent his childhood around the church, but when he became a teenager he forgot about God.

One day, some pirates attacked Patrick's village and took several young people captive, including sixteen-year-old Patrick. Patrick was taken to Ireland and sold as a slave.

Patrick's master was a harsh man who commanded, "From now on, you will tend my sheep."

While tending the sheep on the mountain, Patrick remembered God and humbly said, "Lord, please forgive me for forgetting You."

But God had prepared Patrick for a great mission. Patrick spent six years in slavery. During this time, he prayed passionately to God and learned the Irish language, which was very useful to him in his later mission.

One night, Patrick had a dream in which God said, "Patrick, it is time for you to leave Ireland. Go to the coast. A ship is waiting for you."

Patrick obeyed the Lord. He left secretly and, after a long journey on foot, he got on the ship. Patrick had escaped captivity, just as the Lord said!

After a while, Patrick arrived in Gaul. It was there he met Saint Germanus, who accepted him as a disciple. Patrick studied the priesthood in the monastery in Auxerre and, after a while, became a priest.

Not long after, Patrick had a dream in which an angel came to him bearing many letters. He selected one inscribed 'The Voice of the Irish'. When he opened it, he heard the Irish begging, "Patrick, please come back to us!"

Hearing the dream, Saint Germanus said, "It is God's will!" He supported Patrick to be a bishop and urged him to go to Ireland.

Patrick went to Ireland with some companions and began to preach the Word of God to the Irish.

In this difficult mission, Patrick succeeded Saint Palladius, who had left Ireland because he was terrified by the fierce opposition of a local Irish leader.

Patrick endured many trials and disappointments, but he remained faithful to his calling.

It is said that the local Celtic Druids, who kept the Irish away from God, sent a chieftain named Dichu to kill Patrick.

Dichu drew his sword to strike the saint, but his arm became rigid as a statue.

"Forgive me, holy father!" Dichu begged in great fear.

"Be free, in the name of Jesus Christ!" Patrick said, and so Dichu was released.

Grateful, Dichu offered Patrick shelter where he could perform the holy liturgy.

God's grace was with Patrick. Patrick spoke to the people simply, from the heart, and in their language. He used the shamrock to explain the Holy Trinity.

Patrick said, "There is only one God in three Persons: the Father, the Son, and the Holy Spirit. Just as the three leaves of the shamrock grow from one single stem."

Many Irish believed in God and became Christians, especially young people.

Countless young men and women followed Patrick to become his disciples. Patrick founded monasteries and churches and encouraged young people to take the path to priesthood or monasticism.

One such young woman was Saint Brigid, who founded the first nunnery in Ireland. Through the miracles she performed, St. Bridgit was considered, along with St. Patrick, the protector of Ireland.

God helped Patrick, and Christianity quickly spread throughout Ireland. Even King Leoghaire's family members became Christians, convinced by Patrick's humbleness and the truth of his words.

"Henceforth, you may preach and baptize freely throughout my kingdom," King Leoghaire told Patrick.

Patrick loved the Irish, so he stood against the invaders who attacked them. Patrick wrote a letter to Corotius, the commander of the invaders, condemning the attack and asking him to release the prisoners.

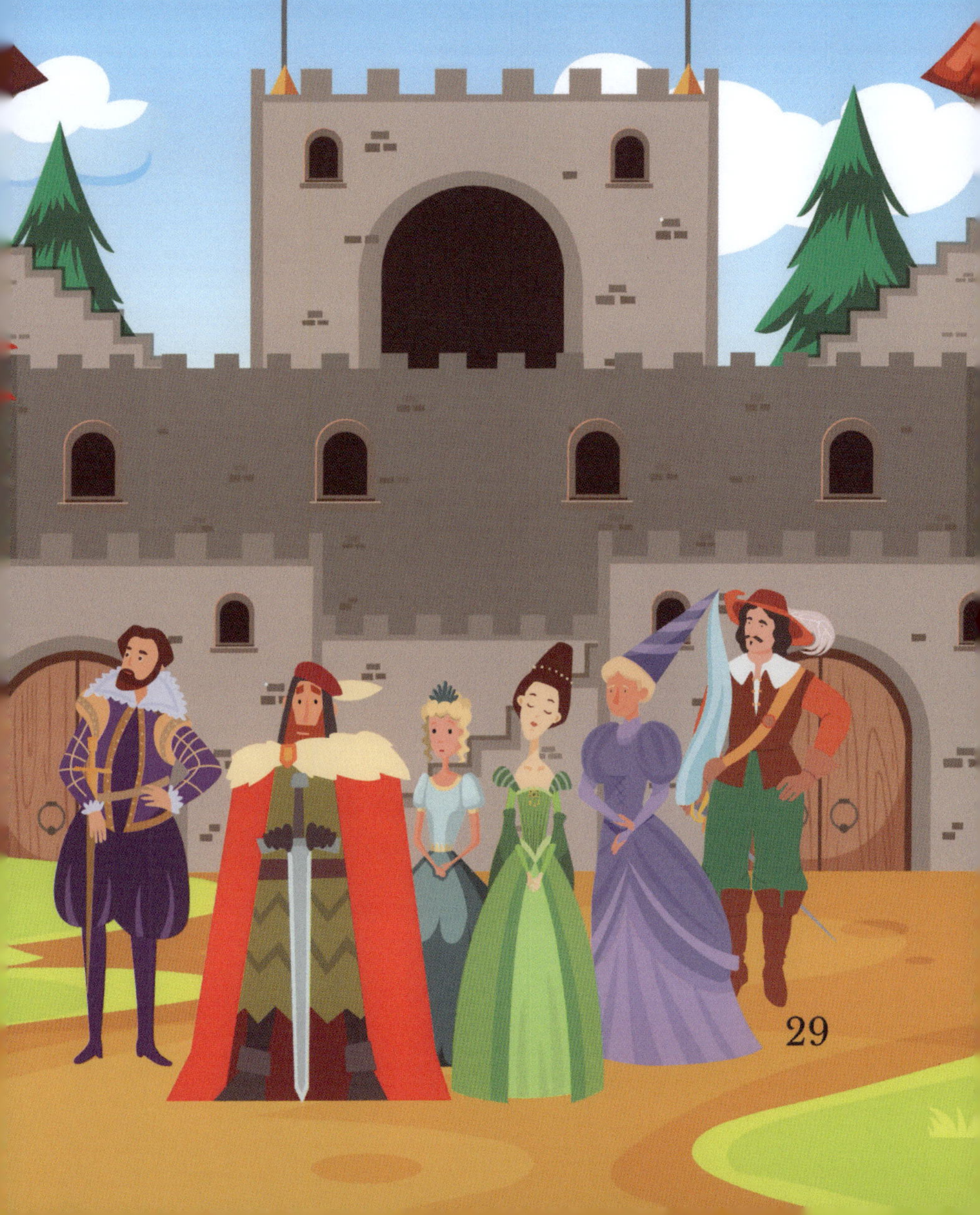

Patrick performed many miracles, but what really moved the hearts of the Irish people was Patrick's humbleness and love for people.

He referred to himself as "the most ignorant and of least account" and gave thanks to God for his success. "I owe it to God's grace that through me so many people should be born again to Him," Patrick wrote.

Shortly before his death, Patrick performed another miracle. Patrick asked God to drive out all the snakes that were troubling the Irish from the island.

When Patrick moved to the Lord in peace, he was surrounded by his disciples.

St. Patrick's Day, celebrated on March 17, is famous all over the world. It is the Irish way of thanking God for sending Saint Patrick to enlighten Ireland on the path to the Kingdom of Heaven.

Printed in Dunstable, United Kingdom

68321507R00018